W9-BBV-057

TRAILBLAZERS of the MODERN WORLD

ROSA PARKS

By Marc Tyler Nobleman

WORLD ALMANAC® LIBRARY

Please visit our web site at: www.worldalmanaclibrary.com
For a free color catalog describing World Almanac® Library's
list of high-quality books and multimedia programs,
call 1-800-848-2928 or fax your request to (414) 332-3567.

Library of Congress Cataloging-in-Publication Data

Nobleman, Marc Tyler.
     Rosa Parks / by Marc Tyler Nobleman.
        p. cm. — (Trailblazers of the modern world)
     Includes bibliographical references and index.
     Summary: A biography of the woman whose refusal to give up her seat on an Alabama bus helped galvanize the civil rights
movement. Features quotations from Parks and others.
     ISBN 0-8368-5071-8 (lib. bdg.)
     ISBN 0-8368-5231-1 (softcover)
     1. Parks, Rosa, 1913–Juvenile literature.   2. African American women—Alabama—Montgomery—Biography—Juvenile
literature.   3. African Americans—Alabama—Montgomery—Biography—Juvenile literature.   4. Civil rights workers—
Alabama—Montgomery—Biography—Juvenile literature.   5. African Americans—Civil rights—Alabama—Montgomery—
History—20th century—Juvenile literature.   6. Segregation in transportation—Alabama—Montgomery—History—20th century—
Juvenile literature.   7. Montgomery (Ala.)—Race relations—Juvenile literature.   8. Montgomery (Ala.)—Biography—Juvenile
literature. [1. Parks, Rosa, 1913-.   2. Civil rights workers.   3. African Americans—Civil rights.   4. African Americans—
Biography.   5. Women—Biography.] I. Title. II. Series.
     F334.M753P386   2002
     323'.092—dc21
     [B]   2001045625

This North American edition first published in 2002 by
World Almanac® Library
330 West Olive Street, Suite 100
Milwaukee, WI 53212 USA

This U.S. edition © 2002 by World Almanac® Library.

An Editorial Directions book
Editor: Lucia Raatma
Designer and page production: Ox and Company
Photo researcher: Dawn Friedman
Indexer: Tim Griffin
World Almanac® Library art direction: Tammy Gruenewald
World Almanac® Library production: Susan Ashley and Jessica L. Yanke

Photo credits: AP/Wide World Photos, cover; AP/Wide World Photos/Lacy Atkins, 4; AP/Wide World Photos/Dave Martin,
5; AP/Wide World Photos/Kevin Glackmeyer, 6; AP/Wide World Photos, 7; Hulton Archive, 8 top; AP/Wide World Photos,
8 bottom, 9 top; Corbis, 9 bottom; AP/Wide World Photos, 10; Corbis, 11, 13, 14, 15, 17 left, 17 right, 19; Hulton Archive,
20; Corbis/Bettmann, 23; AP/Wide World Photos/Gene Herrick, 25; Hulton Archive, 27 top; Corbis/Bettmann, 27 bottom;
AP/Wide World Photos, 28; Corbis, 29; AP/Wide World Photos/John L. Focht, 31; AP/Wide World Photos/Gene Herrick,
33; Hulton Archive, 36; AP/Wide World Photos/RNT, 37; Corbis, 38 top; AP/Wide World Photos, 38 bottom; Corbis, 39,
40 top; Corbis/Bettmann, 40 bottom, 41 top; AP/Wide World Photos/Jim Wells, 41 bottom left; AP/Wide World Photos,
41 bottom right; AP/Wide World Photos/Joe Marquette, 42; AP/Wide World Photos/Laurie Skrivan, 43 top left; AP/Wide
World Photos/Richard Sheinwald, 43 top right; AP/Wide World Photos/Joe Marquette, 43 bottom.

Printed in the United States of America

1 2 3 4 5 6 7 8 9 06 05 04 03 02

TABLE of CONTENTS

Words that appear in the glossary are printed in **boldface**
type the first time they occur in the text.

CHAPTER 1

WOMAN OF PRINCIPLE

"Linking our Past to the New Millennium"

Many dates in American history are remembered for a tragic reason, such as the bombing of Pearl Harbor on December 7, 1941, or a joyous one, such as the signing of the Declaration of Independence on July 4, 1776. Some dates, however, are known for both their painful *and* joyful reasons. Thursday, December 1, 1955, is such a date. It was a difficult day for Rosa Parks when she lived through it, but now it is regarded as one of the most positive days for all Americans in the twentieth century. Even Rosa Parks would agree.

On that day, Rosa Parks, an African-American woman living in the racially **segregated** city of Montgomery, Alabama, was asked to give up her seat on a bus to a white passenger, which was the law then. Like most blacks in America at the time, she had been giving in for many years, and she was tired of it. However, unlike many blacks, who were understandably afraid to protest, Rosa Parks decided to do something, right then and there, to show that the law was wrong. She refused to give up her seat. Within minutes, she was not only ordered to leave the seat but also arrested and taken to jail. Her trial and a bus **boycott** followed immediately after. Many people consider these events to be the birth of the U.S. **civil rights** movement.

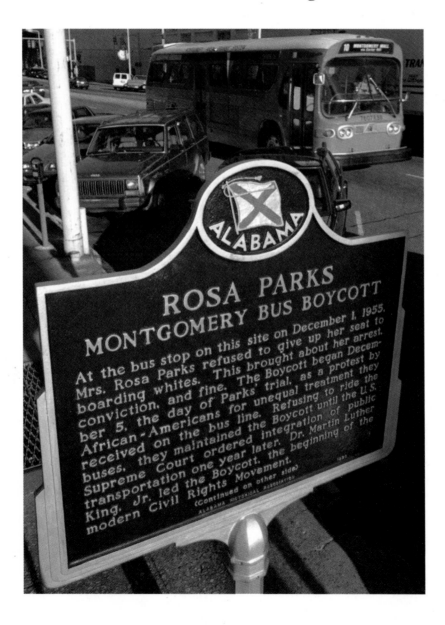

A historic marker at the site of Rosa Parks' arrest in Montgomery

ROSA PARKS
MONTGOMERY BUS BOYCOTT

At the bus stop on this site on December 1, 1955, Mrs. Rosa Parks refused to give up her seat to boarding whites. This brought about her arrest, conviction, and fine. The Boycott began December 5, the day of Parks' trial, as a protest by African-Americans for unequal treatment they received on the bus line. Refusing to ride the buses, they maintained the Boycott until the U.S. Supreme Court ordered integration of public transportation one year later. Dr. Martin Luther King, Jr. led the Boycott, the beginning of the modern Civil Rights Movement.
(Continued on other side)
ALABAMA HISTORICAL ASSOCIATION

Rosa Parks is now one of America's most beloved figures, yet she spent half of her life being treated as a second-class citizen in her own country. She was born poor but raised proud in Alabama. She always did what she felt was right, which was to be respectful and tolerant of everyone, even though the same basic courtesy was rarely shown to her. She certainly did not try to become famous. She did not know that she would be starting a great movement by not budging from her bus seat.

For much of her life, Rosa Parks was forced to move, but she usually didn't mind it. When she was small, she had to move from town to town and school to school, but she was with her mother and that made her happy. As an adult, she had to move from job to job, but she was with her husband, which made it easier.

Rosa Parks did mind, however, when she was forced to move out of her bus seat, and at that time she was alone—but not for long. In fact, staying put on that bus may have been the most important move of her life.

The Rosa Parks Museum is located at the very corner where Parks refused to give up her seat in 1955.

CHAPTER 2

DAUGHTER OF GOODNESS

When Rosa Louise Parks was born in 1913, the Civil War had ended nearly half a century earlier, and World War I would not start for another year. In that sense, the United States seemed at peace. However, for many people, that was not the case. Despite the abolition of slavery by the passage of the **Thirteenth Amendment** to the U.S. Constitution in 1865, **intolerance** was still an accepted part of American life. African-Americans, Jews, Roman Catholics, people from foreign countries, and others were persecuted by many in the white Protestant majority—just because they were different.

Segregation and persecution of African-Americans was especially severe in the South. No one could have known it then, but the birth of one little girl would one day help turn the war against blacks into a war against **racism**.

When Parks was a young woman, blacks were often kept separate from whites in public areas.

BIRTH OF A HEROINE

Rosa Parks was born Rosa Louise McCauley in Tuskegee, Alabama, on February 4, 1913. Her maternal grandparents, Rose and Sylvester Edwards, were former slaves. Her

WAITING ROOM FOR WHITE ONLY ← BY ORDER POLICE DEPT.

The McCauleys lived near the Tuskegee Institute in Alabama.

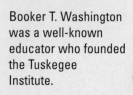

Booker T. Washington was a well-known educator who founded the Tuskegee Institute.

mother, Leona Edwards McCauley, was a teacher, and her father, James McCauley, was a carpenter, bricklayer, and stonemason. Rosa was the first of two children.

Rosa's parents had different reasons for wanting to live in Tuskegee. Rosa's mother knew Tuskegee was the best place in Alabama for black people to get an education, something that was very important to her. Rosa's father expected to find work easily and make more money there, as it was a fairly large town.

They didn't live far from the Tuskegee Institute (now Tuskegee University), a well-known school that was begun in 1881 to serve the educational needs of African-Americans. The school's founder was an influential educator and former slave named Booker T. Washington, and one of the school's most notable professors was George Washington Carver, a black man whose innovative work in the agricultural sciences (particularly with peanuts) made him famous. The Tuskegee Institute offered opportunities that blacks could not get elsewhere in the area, including access to a library. Initially, all the students and teachers were black, but in the 1960s, white students began attending Tuskegee as well. Both blacks and whites felt the school was a symbol of the town's good race relations.

James McCauley soon found that there were better work prospects in the North. First, despite Leona's wishes, he relocated the family to Abbeville, nearly 100 miles (160 kilometers) away, where they lived with his parents. Then he left them there and went even farther north on his own.

Leona McCauley was a strong woman who always wanted to provide as good a life as possible for her family, but she did not want to be in Abbeville to begin with, and even less so with her husband traveling. Also, she was pregnant with Rosa's brother, Sylvester. So, when Rosa was a toddler, Leona moved them to Pine Level, another small town in Alabama. Leona's parents—Rosa's other set of grandparents—had a farm there, and Leona knew they would help her raise the children.

Rosa's father came to Pine Level for a short while but left again when Rosa was two and a half years old. He returned when Rosa was five and Sylvester was three, stayed only several days, then left again. The next time Rosa saw her father, she was a married adult. Her parents did not stay together because they wanted different kinds of lives.

George Washington Carver working in his laboratory at the Tuskegee Institute

A history class at the Tuskegee Institute in 1902

Remembering Her Mother

Young Rosa learned about respect and strength from her mother, Leona. She remembered:

My mother was a teacher in a little school, and she believed in freedom and equality for people, and did not have the notion that we were supposed to live as we did, under legally enforced racial segregation.

In the first part of the twentieth century, many African-Americans made a living by hand-picking cotton for plantation owners.

Rosa's mother and grandparents spent many long hours maintaining their farm, where they raised cows and chickens and grew fruit trees. In addition to working their own land, they labored as field hands on a nearby plantation owned by Moses Hudson, a white man. They also tried hard to teach Rosa and Sylvester to have dignity and strength as well as to have respect for themselves. It must have been a challenge for Leona to teach Rosa about respect. Although the laws and attitudes of white America were not fair to black people at the time, Rosa and Sylvester learned that they were smart and capable of contributing to the lives of others.

What was it like to be black in the South when Rosa was young? African-Americans were mistreated in just about every way imaginable under a system of discrimination known as **Jim Crow laws**. Cities, public build-

ings such as schools, restaurants, hotels, and theaters—plus public transportation such as buses and trains—were divided into sections for "white" and "**colored**" people, and public buildings had separate entrances for blacks and whites as well. Even drinking fountains were separate. In the small town of Pine Level, Rosa didn't see these things, but she felt the rift between whites and blacks in other ways. Most black men could not get very good jobs, no matter how intelligent or hard-working they were, and it was even more difficult for black women.

Despite the laws and attitudes of many white southerners in the Jim Crow era, Rosa didn't grow up thinking that all white people were hateful. She once remembered, "an old, old white lady . . . used to take me fishing. She was real nice and treated us just like everybody else." In 1919, something else happened to Rosa that most children would not think twice about, but Rosa has never forgotten it. Moses Hudson, who owned the big plantation next to her family's farm, came over one day and brought with him a young, white soldier from the North whom he introduced as his son-in-law. The soldier patted Rosa on the head and told her how cute she was. That simple gesture of kindness by a white person

Among other discriminatory restrictions, Jim Crow laws called for separate waiting rooms for blacks and whites.

toward a black person was virtually unheard of at the time, and Moses visibly disapproved of his son-in-law's action. Rosa's family talked about the incident for years to come. Rosa said they remembered the time "a white man treated me like a regular little girl, not a little black girl."

Many if not all of the restrictions against African-

Americans were legal under state (and sometimes even federal) law, so blacks felt that even the government would not protect them from the injustices they were suffering. To make matters worse, the **Ku Klux Klan** (KKK)—an organization made up of white men who hated people who did not share their race or religion—terrified blacks with violence throughout the South. Rosa never saw the Klansmen personally, and they never directly attacked her family, but blacks could never feel safe as long as the KKK was active. The group burned black churches and terrorized, tortured, or even killed black people, often by **lynching**. Rosa's family talked about sleeping in their clothes so they would be ready to escape in case the KKK threatened them during the night. Her grandfather would stay up with his shotgun close at hand, ready to protect his family if the worst happened. Rosa remembers him saying, "I don't know how long I would last if they came breaking in here, but I'm getting the first one who comes through the door."

Racial restrictions, as well as the terror of the KKK, affected Rosa McCauley, but one rule in particular was her destiny. More than thirty years in the future, her seemingly small resistance to one specific restriction would prove to be critical in the nationwide struggle for black equality—and in U.S. history.

Grandfather Sylvester

Growing up without a father, Rosa relied on her grandfather as a male role model. He protected the family, and he wanted the best for Rosa. In *Rosa Parks: My Story*, she wrote:

The one thing he wanted most of all was for none of his children or anyone related to him to ever have to cook or clean for whites. He wanted all his children to be educated so they wouldn't have to do that kind of work.

The Ku Klux Klan

The Ku Klux Klan (KKK) is an organization that was founded by former Confederate army officers in Tennessee in 1866. It was conceived as a social club, but racism soon became its defining characteristic. The group's mission was to resist new governments set up in the South after the Civil War, during the rebuilding process called Reconstruction. Klan members believed that whites were superior to all others, particularly blacks, and that former white slaveholders should retain control in the South. They expressed their unjust views using violence, often torturing and murdering blacks and anyone who supported them. One of their tactics was burning crosses near the homes of people whom they wished to intimidate. The Klan was disbanded later in the 1800s but reformed in 1915, two years after Rosa Parks was born. To join, a man had to be white, Protestant, and American-born. The KKK expanded quickly after World War I but membership shrank in the 1930s. In the 1950s and 1960s, scattered groups calling themselves KKK terrorized blacks and civil-rights activists, more heavily in the South. The KKK exists today, but they do not have the power they once did. Thanks to people like Rosa Parks, we live in a more equal world than ever before. The brutal and ignorant ways of the KKK are no longer tolerated by the majority.

CHAPTER 3

STUDENT OF EQUALITY

Many southern schools for blacks lacked the books and supplies that white schools had.

Leona McCauley taught Rosa to read at home. In 1918, Rosa began attending school in Pine Level in the type of old, one-room schoolhouse for black children that was common in the South. Many of these schools had no desks, and they relied on a single stove for warmth. Rosa had to pass the new, big school for whites on her long walk to her small, run-down school. One school she attended was 8 miles (13 km) away.

FROM SCHOOL TO SCHOOL

In Pine Level, classes for black children stopped at sixth grade, so in 1924, at age eleven, Rosa had to leave her small town to continue her education in the city of Montgomery, 30 miles (48 km) away. She began attending Montgomery Industrial School for Girls, a private school founded by liberal women from the North. In spite of its formal name, most students knew it as Miss White's School for Girls because of its principal and co-founder, Alice L. White. At the school, both co-founders and all the teachers were white, while all the students were black. In Pine Level, the school for African-

Americans was open only five months of the year, while the white school was open nine months of the year. At Miss White's, school was also in session nine months of the year. Unlike the one-room schools Rosa was used to, Miss White's was a three-story building. Leona paid for Rosa's school for a while, but then Rosa cleaned classrooms in exchange for her tuition. She attended the all-black Booker T. Washington Junior High for ninth grade, followed by the Alabama State Teachers' College for Negroes for tenth and the beginning of eleventh grade. Both of those schools were also in Montgomery.

In 1929, at age sixteen, Rosa left school and returned to Pine Level because her grandmother Rose got sick. About a month later, her grandmother died, and

After sixth grade, Rosa McCauley began attending school in the larger city of Montgomery, Alabama.

Rosa's Education

Though Rosa attended a number of schools, the memory of her first school stayed with her throughout her life. She wrote:

The first school I attended was a small building that went from first to sixth grade. There was one teacher for all of the students. There could be anywhere from fifty to sixty students of all different ages. From five or six years old to [students] in their teens. We went to school five months out of the year. The rest of the time young people would be available to work on the farm. The parents had to buy whatever the student used. Often, if your family couldn't afford it, you had no access to books, pencils, whatever. However, often the children would share. I liked to read all sorts of stories, like fairy tales—Little Red Riding Hood, Mother Goose. I read very often.

Rosa got a job in a shirt factory in Montgomery instead of going back to school. Soon her mother got sick, and once again Rosa returned to Pine Level to care for her until she got better. Rosa would finish high school, but she would get married first.

LOVE IN ALABAMA

A mutual friend introduced Rosa to a Montgomery barber named Raymond Parks. He liked Rosa from the start, but she didn't feel the same—not right away. Raymond wasn't just a barber, however. He was also an **activist** for civil rights, the first one Rosa had ever met. Activism was not easy work for anybody, and certainly not for a black man, but especially not for a light-skinned black man like Raymond.

The definitions of who was "black" or "white" were complicated, but essentially, if a person had any African ancestry, he was considered black, no matter how "white" (or tan or yellow or pink) his skin appeared. Imagine how you would feel if someone who thought you were white had been nice to you and suddenly began treating you badly when you said you were actually black. Raymond had to deal with such insulting situations regularly. In fact, after he and Rosa met in the city, Raymond drove out to Pine Level to pay her a visit, and when he couldn't find her house, a black neighbor would not tell him where it was because he looked white. Everyone knew that it

The Scottsboro Boys

A major civil rights trial of the 1930s was the Scottsboro case. In this case, nine young African-American men (above left; shown protected by the National Guard) were all accused of sexually assaulting two white women on a train in Scottsboro, Alabama, in 1931. They had been on the train, and a fight had broken out when a group of whites began throwing rocks at the blacks, but there was no medical evidence of rape. Even so, an all-white jury sentenced the youngest of them, who was thirteen, to life in prison, and the rest to the electric chair. People around the world followed the case, and many groups protested the ruling (above right). Raymond was one of many who believed the Scottsboro boys were innocent, and for many years he and a small group of others were secretly raising funds for their court fees. He would sometimes host Scottsboro defense committee meetings at his and Rosa's home. It took great courage to support the defendants because he or Rosa could have been killed for their efforts. Members of the KKK or other **vigilantes** could easily have set their house on fire or attacked them in other ways. Despite this danger, Raymond knew that supporting the Scottsboro boys was the right thing to do. Even though Rosa was scared, she knew it, too. Eventually, one of the two white women revealed that she had falsely accused the boys. Because of successful appeals and overturns by the U.S. Supreme Court, none of the Scottsboro boys was put to death, but five served long prison terms.

meant trouble if a white person was looking for a black person.

Luckily, Raymond soon found the right house, and Leona invited him in. Rosa was shy at first, but Raymond—or Parks, as everyone called him—came back to see Rosa often enough that she realized what a good person he was. It was unusual for a black man to have a car of his own, but Parks did, and he took Rosa on drives during which they shared stories of their childhoods. The stories, of course, were not always happy ones since Parks was also raised in the segregated South, and in an all-white neighborhood on top of it. Eventually, they fell in love.

Rosa and Raymond were married in December 1932 at Leona's home in Pine Level.

BECOMING AN ACTIVIST

The Parkses moved to Montgomery during the 1930s. At this time, the United States was experiencing the **Great Depression**, a period marked by massive unemployment and poverty. Raymond had little formal schooling himself, but he was very supportive of Rosa when she went back to school while he continued to work as a barber. Rosa received her high school diploma in 1933, when she was twenty. She couldn't get work as a secretary because whites generally wouldn't hire blacks, and blacks usually did not hold positions that required such support staff. So Rosa took a respectable job as a seamstress at Montgomery Fair Department Store, considered the best in the city.

In 1943, Rosa joined the Montgomery chapter of the National Association for the Advancement of Colored People (NAACP), an organization founded in 1909 whose mission is to peacefully promote equality for blacks. Her husband had been a member since before she met him. Parks was one of the first women in

Montgomery to become a member. The beliefs she held that prompted her to join were not new. Parks had known since childhood that the way white people treated black people was inexcusable and needed to be changed. The NAACP did not have too many victories in the 1940s and early 1950s in seeking justice, but they were making it known that people cared about improving the situation for African-Americans. Although Parks couldn't get a secretarial job in the city, she did serve as secretary of the Montgomery branch of the NAACP. It didn't earn her any money, but it would ultimately earn her something much more valuable.

A 1934 NAACP protest against the practice of lynching

CHAPTER 4

CHAMPION FOR FREEDOM

Rosa and Raymond Parks were active in promoting voter registration for black citizens. Rosa joined the Montgomery Voters' League, a group that motivated black people to register to vote. Rosa believed that voting is one of the most sacred rights of Americans, and she worked hard to ensure that right. A man named Edgar Daniel (E. D.) Nixon was very influential in this effort in Montgomery. Nixon was a dignified man and a leader who had many roles in the city's black community. He was a railroad porter, or a person who assists passengers in sleeping cars on trains, and he was president of the local branch of a black railroad workers' union. He also held the position of president of both the Montgomery and the state chapters of the NAACP. Rosa helped out in Nixon's office by typing letters.

The NAACP held a number of peaceful protests during the civil rights movement.

THE GIFT OF THE VOTE

The **Fourteenth Amendment** and the **Fifteenth Amendment** to the Constitution (ratified in 1868 and 1870, respectively) had given every male born in the United States the right to vote regardless of "race, color, or previous condition of servitude," yet many laws and practices made it difficult for blacks to vote. (Women, white and black, finally obtained the right to vote in 1920.) Racist Americans created one obstacle after another to prevent African-Americans from voting, despite what the Constitution allowed.

One obstacle was the **poll tax**. Legislatures in certain states would require blacks to pay this tax of $1.50 per year at the voting site. Considering that wages for black people were often extremely low, this tax was a financial burden for many of them. Also, the poll tax was retroactive to age twenty-one, meaning a voter would have to pay $1.50 per year for *every* year that had passed since the voter's twenty-first birthday. Another obstacle was the "literacy test." Before they could vote, many people were forced to take this test about the Constitution and the U.S. government. Whites passed automatically, but blacks were often failed without being given a reason.

One of those who "failed" was Rosa Parks, or at least that's what she was told. The first time she tried to register, in 1943, she took the test but never received the registration certificate in the mail. The second time she tried, she was told she did not pass—case closed. Parks was fairly sure she *had* passed but figured no one would listen if she disputed

On Discrimination

Parks remembered what it was like to be black during this difficult time in U.S. history. She wrote:

As an adult, I would go home thirsty on a hot summer day rather than take a drink from the "colored only" fountain. I would not be a part of an unjust system that was designed to make me feel inferior.

the decision. The third time, however, she planned ahead. Parks copied the twenty-one test questions and her answers onto another sheet of paper so she could show later on that she was correct. She never had to prove it, however, because that time, her certificate did arrive in the mail. Rosa Parks was a registered voter, but she still had to pay her poll tax, of course.

RULES OF THE BUS

On public buses in the South, the first ten seats were reserved for white passengers. It was understood that blacks had to move to the back, even if the bus was empty, and even in the back, they were not guaranteed a seat. If their designated front section was full, whites had preferential status for the back seats, too. The system was unfair, but it was also impractical. Blacks accounted for more than two-thirds of the passengers, yet they had to squeeze into the back of the bus no matter what. Their majority would soon become an instrumental tool in forcing the system to change.

At that time, it was common for the white drivers to ask a black person who had already paid the fare at the front door to get off the bus and reenter through the back door. This practice was done to spare the white passengers the "discomfort" of a black person walking by them. Although it's hard to believe, some drivers carried guns to emphasize that it was less of a request and more of a demand. Also, after they made a black person who paid the fare exit and go around, some drivers would then pull away before he or she could get back on the bus.

Besides trying to register to vote and failing, Parks had another degrading first in 1943. She was forced off a city bus for the first time. It was a winter day. The driver's name was James Blake. Parks paid her fare and walked past the white section. She turned around to see Blake standing and staring at her. He told her to get off and come back on through the back door, but she politely said that she had already worked her way through the crowded bus and didn't see why she should have to do it again.

Blake grabbed her coat sleeve ("not my arm," Parks later specified) and pulled her toward the front. Her purse dropped, and she sat in a white seat for a moment to pick it up. This enraged Blake, who said, "Get off my bus." He looked angry enough to strike her.

A segregated city bus in Montgomery in the early 1950s

Rosa Parks on Self-Esteem

The respect that Rosa Parks had for herself and for others was instilled in her as a child. She recalled:

My mother and grandmother made sure the mean words of some of the white children I came in contact with did not make me feel bad about myself. They told me of the strength of our ancestors, who had endured slavery. They reminded me of the love of God that was always with me. They shared their dreams of hope that made them look forward to a new world based on equality and justice. I have never forgotten their dreams for me and their words of encouragement. Their dreams live inside of me, through good times and bad.

"I will get off," Rosa Parks said. "I know one thing. You better not hit me."

Blake didn't, and as Parks got off she heard a fellow African-American say, "How come she don't go around and get in the back?" Black people were so used to bad treatment that many thought it was pointless to resist, and they were frustrated with those who tried to make changes.

Rather than get on Blake's bus again, Parks waited for the next one and vowed she would always check the driver first before entering another bus. She didn't want to encounter James Blake again.

INSPIRATION TO MANY

Working with E. D. Nixon was a challenging and positive experience for Rosa Parks. Although Nixon was a supporter of equal rights for blacks, like many men of the era, he felt that women "don't need to be nowhere but in the kitchen." Naturally, Parks didn't agree with that, and when she asked, "Well, what about me?" he said he needed a secretary and Parks was a good one. Nixon had his flaws, but he was determined to put an end to the suffering of African-Americans.

E. D. Nixon (left) employed Rosa Parks and also supported her during her court appearances.

As with everything else she did, Parks worked very hard for Nixon, and soon her duties expanded beyond standard secretarial work. She still worked full days as a seamstress, but she always put in time at Nixon's office during her lunch hour, at night, and on weekends. Because he was a railroad porter, Nixon was away often, and during those times Parks was in charge. She interviewed African-Americans who came to file reports of abuse and compiled reports based on evidence. Nixon hired Parks to help with other projects for the black cause in addition to what the NAACP did, and through that, Parks met many state and national leaders. She also knew the community very well, and they knew her.

By 1949, Parks was adviser to the NAACP Youth Council. She and Raymond never had children of their own, but Rosa has always loved guiding young people so much that she once said, "I consider all children as mine." Like most of Montgomery's facilities, the library was divided into a main library and a "colored" library—a small branch with a limited selection of books and located far from the city's center. If a student wanted a book that the colored library didn't have, the colored library would have to request it from the main library and the student would have to come back to the colored library to pick it up. It was an offensive and irrational process. Parks organized a program in which high school students who were in the Youth Council would repeatedly go to the main library and explain that the colored library was too far away. This attempt to change the system was noble, but the Youth Council students were consistently turned down.

Through Nixon, Parks met Virginia and Clifford Durr in 1954. The Durrs were a local white couple who supported black rights. Clifford was one of the few white lawyers in Montgomery who would work with African-Americans, and because of that, the Durrs did not have many white friends—or clients. Parks said that Virginia, who was born and raised in Birmingham, Alabama, "managed to overcome all the racism with which she grew up." (Incidentally, Virginia Durr's sister was married to Hugo Black, a Supreme Court justice.) Rosa and Virginia became good friends.

Meanwhile, Fred Gray, a black man who had left his home state of Alabama to go to law school, returned to the city with his degree. Because of his skin color, he hadn't had the option of studying in Alabama even if he wanted to, so he had studied in the North. Once back in Montgomery, he set up a law practice because he, too, believed that there was much work to be done to help black people in the South. Just as she was drawn to E. D. Nixon because of his beliefs, Parks began helping out at Fred Gray's office as well.

Fred Gray was an attorney in Montgomery.

Brown v. the Board of Education

In 1954, the U.S. Supreme Court handed down a landmark decision in *Brown v. the Board of Education of Topeka.* In the case, the court ruled that the "separate but equal" policy of racially divided public schools was **unconstitutional** and that those schools must be **integrated**. In other words, white children and black children must attend school together. However, like any large task, that was much easier said than done. Such a major change could not happen overnight, especially since so many still opposed it.

Virginia told Rosa about a workshop that was being held at the Highlander Folk School in Tennessee, a school that trained civil rights leaders. In the summer of 1955, Parks went to the ten-day workshop about ending racial segregation and liked what she learned so much that she was didn't want to leave. Both blacks and whites studied there, and Parks later said that it was the first time in her life she had been in an environment where she didn't feel any hostility from white people. Myles Horton, the founder of Highlander, later said that he was very proud that Rosa Parks attended his school.

With renewed hope for a better future, Rosa Parks returned to Montgomery.

LOOKING FOR MR. OR MS. RIGHT

The three lawyers that led the fight to end segregation in public schools: George E. C. Hayes (left), Thurgood Marshall (center), and James Nabrit (right)

In December 1949, a black college professor named Jo Ann Robinson had an experience with an aggressive white bus driver, which was similar to Rosa's 1943 run-in with James Blake. Robinson had accidentally sat in a white seat, was shouted at, and quickly got off the bus. Three years earlier, in 1946, she helped found the Women's Political Council (WPC), and the group made plans to push for a bus boycott—as Robinson explained it, "when the time was ripe and the people were ready." She and others knew that in general

Rosa Parks on *Brown v. the Board of Education*

After the U.S. Supreme Court handed down its history-making decision, Rosa Parks remembered the reaction in the African-American community.

You can't imagine the rejoicing among black people, and some white people, when the Supreme Court decision came down in May 1954. The Court had said that separate education could not be equal, and many of us saw how the same idea applied to other things, like public transportation.

whites could afford cars more easily than blacks, so many more blacks than whites used the bus every day. If blacks united to boycott the buses, the effect would be financially damaging for the bus companies. More important, it would send a strong message about what was fair and what was not.

The NAACP was also looking for the right time to take action against the city by filing a lawsuit for its unjust bus segregation. In particular, they were waiting for the arrest of a person—any person—who could be an effective spokesperson when the case went to trial.

In spring of 1955, a fifteen-year-old black girl named Claudette Colvin was arrested for refusing to surrender her seat in the white section of a bus. Later that year, two other women were arrested for similar "offenses." Unfortunately, for varying reasons, none of them fit the description of the type of person the NAACP and the WPC needed to win the case. Neither group, however, would go so far as to send a person onto the bus with the intention of being arrested on purpose.

CRUSADER AGAINST INJUSTICE

It was December 1, 1955, and Rosa Parks was forty-two years old. She was still employed as an assistant tailor at Montgomery Fair Department Store. That day after work, she waited at a bus stop on Cleveland Avenue, so deep in thought about an upcoming meeting that she didn't pay attention to the driver of the bus.

At the National Civil Rights Museum in Memphis, Tennessee, visitors can sit on a real Montgomery city bus on display, view the figure of Rosa Parks, and hear a recording of a bus driver ordering her to give up her seat.

BREAKING THE RULES

As she got on, Parks paid the ten-cent fare, then noticed that the driver was James Blake, the man who had been so cruel to her on a bus twelve years before.

Although the bus was crowded, a seat past the white section in the middle had somehow remained vacant, and Parks sat there beside three other black people. At the next stop, which was a local attraction called the Empire Theater, enough whites boarded to fill their entire section—with one white man left standing.

To all the people in Rosa's row, Blake said, "Let me have those front seats."

No one moved.

Blake said it again, but more forcefully, and three of the four got up. Rosa Parks didn't. In fact, she slid over to the window seat.

She had paid the same fare as everyone else and didn't see how getting up would help the black cause. Blake, of course, didn't see it the same way.

He asked Parks if she was going to get up.

"No," she said.

"Well, I'm going to have you arrested," Blake said.

"You may do that," Rosa Parks said.

So he did.

THE RIGHT SEAT

"On that Thursday evening in December of 1955, I felt the presence of God on the bus and heard His quiet voice as I sat there waiting for the police to take me to the station. There were people on the bus that knew me, but no one said a word to help or encourage me. I was lonely, but I was at peace. The voice of God told me that He was at my side," Parks said later.

Some other passengers hurried off the bus. Those who didn't leave stayed quiet. Two policemen arrived. One asked why Parks didn't stand up.

"Why do you all push us around?" Rosa said.

Parks remembers the exact words of his response. "I don't know, but the law is the law and you're under arrest."

Four decades after the incident, Parks said, "People have said over the years that the reason I did not give up my seat was because I was tired. I did not think of being physically tired. My feet were not hurting. I was tired in a different way. I was tired of seeing so many men being treated as boys and not called by their proper names or titles. I was tired of seeing children and women mistreated and disrespected because of the color of their skin. I was tired of Jim Crow laws, of legally enforced racial segregation. I thought of the pain and the years of mistreatment that my people had suffered. I felt that way every day. December 1, 1955, was no different. Fear was the last thing I thought of that day. I put my trust in the Lord for guidance and help to endure whatever I had to face. I knew I was sitting in the right seat."

Rosa Parks being fingerprinted by a Montgomery police officer

Rosa Parks was escorted off the bus and into American history, though at the time she only felt as though she was going to jail.

Making History

Rosa Parks did not intend to make history on that December day in 1955. She recalled:

I did not get on the bus to get arrested; I got on the bus to go home. Getting arrested was one of the worst days of my life. I had no idea that history was being made. I was just tired of giving in. Somehow, I felt that what I did was right by standing up to that bus driver. I did not think about the consequences. I knew that I could have been lynched, manhandled, or beaten when the police came. I chose not to move, because I was right. When I made that decision, I knew that I had the strength of God and my ancestors with me.

Throughout the whole ordeal, Rosa stayed calm and tried not to be frightened. She didn't remain in jail for very long, but while she was there, she received little respect. She was not allowed a drink of water, but she was allowed to call home and speak with Raymond and Leona. She told the story and assured them that the police had not beaten her, but it was not the time to tell them that they weren't nice to her, either. Raymond said he would come right away.

Word of Rosa's arrest spread fast in the community. E. D. Nixon had found out and called the jail to find out what the charge was, but because he was black they wouldn't tell him. He called Fred Gray for help, but he wasn't home. Then he called Clifford Durr, who, being a white lawyer, was able to find out that Rosa was arrested for violation of segregation laws.

Virginia Durr was the first familiar face Rosa saw when she was let out of the cell. Virginia had tears in her eyes. Rosa remembers that Virginia hugged and kissed her "as if we were sisters." Clifford and Nixon were with her, and Raymond, who did not have a car and had to wait for a ride, arrived not long after. Rosa's court date was set for the following Monday, December 5, and the group left with heavy emotion.

At the Parks' home, Clifford and Nixon said Rosa's case could be the one they needed to take the segregation issue to court—even to the U.S. Supreme Court—if she was willing. Although Raymond and Leona were worried about Rosa's safety, they ultimately supported her decision. She agreed. She knew it was the right thing to do.

Elsewhere in Montgomery, Jo Ann Robinson also knew that with Rosa's arrest, the time had come to launch a bus boycott and demand that the policies of prejudice be removed. It would be nearly impossible for whites to manipulate the facts about Rosa Parks to make her look bad in any way. She lived an exemplary life. She was intelligent and happily married, and she had a good job. She was well known and well liked in the community, and although no one came to her defense on the bus, it was possible that as a group, the blacks of Montgomery would come to their own defense *off* the bus. To maximize the boycott's effect, however, Robinson knew it had to happen the same day that Parks appeared in court, to show support for her.

Announcing the Boycott

Below is an abridged version of the flyer that was created to announce the famous Montgomery bus boycott:

This is for Monday, December 5, 1955. Another Negro woman has been arrested and thrown into jail because she refused to get up out of her seat on the bus and give it to a white person.... This has to be stopped.... The next time it may be you, or your daughter, or mother. This woman's case will come up on Monday. We are, therefore, asking every Negro to stay off the buses Monday in protest of the arrest and trial.... You can afford to stay out of school for one day. If you work, take a cab, or walk. But please, children and grown-ups, don't ride the bus at all on Monday. Please stay off all buses Monday.

That was Monday, less than three days away. In one short weekend, news of the boycott had to reach Montgomery's entire black population of 50,000 people.

SPRINGING INTO ACTION

Martin Luther King, Jr., played a key role in the Montgomery Bus Boycott.

Fred Gray called Jo Ann Robinson at 11:30 that Thursday night, and they discussed the plan. Jo Ann would quickly write up the notice and copy it at the college where she worked. The WPC had already prepared a distribution procedure for just such a situation, and with their help, Jo Ann delivered 35,000 notices to schools and businesses of all sorts by Friday morning. They had to stay up all night to do it, but it was worth the effort.

Meanwhile, Nixon called black ministers around town to ask them to make the announcement in church on Sunday. Religious leaders were perhaps the most reliable way to get out any message, as churches were the only large meeting places where African-Americans met regularly without much fear of interruption.

One of the ministers Nixon called was new in town. His congregation was the Dexter Avenue Baptist Church. The minister was twenty-six years old, and his name was Dr. Martin Luther King, Jr.

CHAPTER 7

MOTHER OF A MOVEMENT

W hen it started, nobody knew how long the bus boycott would last. The organizers instructed blacks only to boycott on Monday and explained that they would convene Monday night to decide what to do next.

THE BOYCOTT AND BEYOND

Monday came. Blacks carpooled to work, and black taxi-cab drivers lowered their fares to ten cents a trip, the same as it would cost someone to ride the bus. Observers noted that almost no blacks rode the buses that day. Sure enough, the African-American community was uniting.

One of the many church-operated vehicles that helped transport African-Americans during the bus boycott

Rosa Parks with Charles Langford, one of the attorneys who represented her

A large crowd had gathered at the courthouse, including many members of the NAACP Youth Council. As Rosa Parks arrived, looking confident and well dressed, someone was heard saying, "They've messed with the wrong one now."

Fred Gray, along with attorney Charles Langford, represented Parks at the trial. She was convicted and fined a total of $14, and her lawyers appealed.

Later that day, an organization called the Montgomery Improvement Association was formed to regulate the boycott. Dr. Martin Luther King, Jr., already gaining a reputation as a powerful speaker, was named president, and E. D. Nixon was treasurer. Robinson, Gray, and Rosa Parks were on the executive board. At a meeting that night, the group made a list of their three requests for the city and the bus companies: change the law that says black passengers must give up their seats for white passengers; instruct drivers to be courteous to all passengers; and hire black drivers. Although the city did not agree to these requests, change was in the air.

On November 13, 1956, the U.S. Supreme Court made a remarkable ruling. It stated that segregation on Alabama transportation was illegal. This was incredible

One of the many buses that sat empty during the boycott

Martin Luther King, Jr., and the Boycott

On the night of December 5, 1955, after the first day of the Montgomery Bus Boycott, Martin Luther King, Jr., had these words for the crowd he addressed:

There comes a time that people get tired. We are here this evening to say to those who have mistreated us so long that we are tired—tired of being segregated and humiliated; tired of being kicked about by the brutal feet of oppression.... For many years we have shown amazing patience. We have sometimes given our white brothers the feeling that we like the way we are being treated. But we come here tonight to be saved from that patience that makes us patient with anything less than freedom and justice.... [w]hen the history books are written in future generations the historians will pause and say, "There lived a great people—a black people—who injected new meaning and dignity into the veins of civilization."

news, but Parks remembered, "We stayed off the buses until it was official." Slightly more than a month later, the written order from the Supreme Court arrived, and the boycott was finally over.

The Montgomery Bus Boycott lasted through December 20, 1956—a staggering 381 days. For more than a year, blacks banded together and found alternate

After the Supreme Court ruling, segregation signs were removed from all public buses.

In this photograph of Parks after the Supreme Court decision, she sits on a city bus with a white man behind her.

ways of travel, even if meant inconvenience, and despite threats and attacks. It hadn't been easy, but by carrying out this boycott, they broke down a barrier that extended far beyond inconvenience: segregation. The civil rights movement had begun, and it had begun to spread into other parts of the country.

The day after the boycott ended, photographers came to take pictures of Rosa Parks sitting on a bus. In the photos, a white man was seated behind her.

FROM ACTIVIST TO LEGEND

In 1957, Rosa and Raymond Parks and Rosa's mother, Leona, moved to Detroit. Rosa's brother, Sylvester, had lived there since he returned from service in World War II (1939–1945). The Parkses wanted to live near Sylvester, and they also realized it was time to leave Alabama. Since the boycott, they had been receiving threatening phone calls, presumably from those who felt they were causing trouble.

Parks stayed active in the civil rights movement, even when situations were tense or disappointing. A lot of intolerance, confusion, and struggle lay ahead—for Rosa Parks and for all African-Americans.

In 1963, Parks was there when King gave his moving "I Have a Dream" speech in Washington, D.C. She was there when blacks marched to protest voting discrimination in Selma, Alabama, in 1965. Even today, it's a good bet that she will be there any time someone is fighting for

Because of Rosa Parks' courage, buses all over the United States became integrated.

equality. In the hearts and minds of supporters of civil rights, she will be there in spirit, if not in person.

In 1965, Parks took a job in the Detroit office of newly elected Democratic congressman John Conyers, Jr. Three years later, when Dr. King was assassinated, Rosa and her mother wept in each other's arms.

As the years passed, Rosa experienced great honor as well as great loss. In 1977, both Raymond and Sylvester died. Two years later, her mother, Leona, died, too. In 1988, Parks retired from Conyers' office, but she did not stop working. Among other things, she founded the Rosa and Raymond Parks Institute for Self Development, whose purpose is to help young people realize their potential.

Throughout her life, Parks has received dozens of awards, degrees, and honors from organizations and universities around the world. In 1965, Cleveland Avenue in Montgomery was renamed Rosa Parks Boulevard; in 1996, President Bill Clinton bestowed on Rosa Parks the Presidential Medal of Freedom; and in 1999, Parks was honored with the Congressional Gold Medal, the highest recognition a United States civilian can receive. On December 1, 2000, the Rosa L. Parks Library and Museum was dedicated at Troy State University in Montgomery, Alabama.

Martin Luther King, Jr., during the historic civil rights march on Washington in 1963

below left: Congressman John Conyers, Jr., of Michigan gave Parks a job when she moved to Detroit.

below right: Parks while working in Congressman Conyers' office

The Rosa and Raymond Parks Institute for Self Development

The Rosa and Raymond Parks Institute for Self Development was founded in February 1987 by Rosa Parks and Elaine Eason Steele, in honor of Raymond Parks. Its mission is as follows:

We encourage youth to reach their highest potential through the Rosa Parks philosophy of "Quiet Strength." Quiet Strength incorporates life skills that demonstrate dignity with pride, courage with perseverance and power with discipline in the comfortable environment of peace.

Representative Julia Carson of Indiana proudly unveiling the Rosa Parks Congressional Gold Medal in 1999

Throughout her lifetime, Rosa Parks has met with many prominent leaders, including Pope John Paul II.

Today, Rosa Parks would not say she is a legend, nor would she say that such a title is important. She merely wants all people to be free and to live by the golden rule: to act toward others the way you want them to act toward you.

Rosa Parks taking time to read one of her biographies to some children in Detroit in 1997

The Presidential Medal of Freedom

At the Presidential Medal of Freedom awards ceremony, on September 9, 1996, President Bill Clinton had this to say:

When Rosa Parks refused to give up her seat to a white man on an Alabama bus 40 years ago, she ignited the single most significant social movement in American history. When she sat down on the bus, she stood up for the American ideals of equality and justice and demanded that the rest of us do the same. When our descendants look back in time to trace the fight for freedom, Rosa Parks will stand among our nation's greatest patriots, the legendary figures whose courage sustained us and pushed us forward. She is, and continues to be, a national treasure.

TIMELINE

1913	Rosa McCauley is born on February 4 in Tuskegee, Alabama
1918	Begins school in Pine Level, Alabama
1924	Attends school in Montgomery, Alabama
1929	Leaves school to care for her grandmother
1932	Marries Raymond Parks
1943	Serves as secretary of the NAACP in Montgomery
1943	Is removed from a city bus for entering through the front
1949	Works with NAACP Youth Council
1955	On December 1, is arrested for refusing to give up her bus seat to a white passenger; on December 5, appears in court and is found guilty of violating segregation laws; the Montgomery Bus Boycott begins
1956	The Supreme Court rules that bus segregation is illegal, and the boycott ends
1957	Parks moves to Detroit with her husband and mother
1963	Hears Dr. Martin Luther King, Jr., speak at the civil rights march in Washington, D.C.
1965	Begins working for Michigan congressman John Conyers, Jr.
1977	Both Raymond Parks and (brother) Sylvester McCauley die
1979	Leona McCauley dies
1987	Co-founds the Rosa and Raymond Parks Institute for Self Development
1988	Retires from the office of Congressman Conyers
1996	Receives the Presidential Medal of Freedom
1999	Receives the Congressional Gold Medal
2000	Attends the dedication of the Rosa L. Parks Library and Museum

GLOSSARY

activist: a person who supports and works for a controversial issue

boycott: a protest in which a group refuses to use a particular service to indicate that they want a change in an unfair practice

civil rights: the freedoms and privileges guaranteed to citizens by the United States Constitution

colored: a once accepted but now derogatory term for an African-American

Fifteenth Amendment: a change to the U.S. Constitution that guaranteed the right to vote could not be denied on the basis of race, 1870

Fourteenth Amendment: a change to the U.S. Constitution that guaranteed anyone (including blacks) born in the United States to be both a national and a state citizen who could not be deprived of life, liberty, or property, without due process of law, 1868

Great Depression: a period in U.S. history—beginning in 1929 and extending through the early 1940s—marked by unemployment and poverty

integrated: brought together, particularly once-divided racial groups

intolerance: unwillingness to grant equal rights and freedoms

Jim Crow laws: the corrupt system of discrimination against black people that was once in place in the American South; the laws enforced the separation of races in many public places such as waiting rooms, trains, buses, and movie theaters; the laws were named for a nineteenth-century vaudeville character who appeared in black face

Ku Klux Klan: a society of white Christians who believe they are superior to all other races and religions

lynching: the illegal execution of a person, often by a gang of people, and usually by hanging

poll tax: the fee that was often required in order to vote, now abolished

racism: mistreatment of a group of people based upon their race

segregated: separated into more than one group, particularly racial groups

Thirteenth Amendment: a change to the U.S. Constitution that called for the end of slavery, 1865

unconstitutional: illegal; commonly describes a ruling that is not consistent with the purpose of the U.S. Constitution

vigilantes: people who carry out what they perceive to be justice, without the support of government or police

TO FIND OUT MORE

BOOKS

Brandt, Keith. *Rosa Parks: Fight for Freedom.* New York: Troll, 1993.

Greenfield, Eloise. *Rosa Parks.* New York: HarperCollins, 1996.

Hull, Mary. *Rosa Parks (Black Americans of Achievement).* Broomall, Penn.: Chelsea House Publishers, 1994.

Parks, Rosa, with Jim Haskins. *Rosa Parks: My Story.* New York: Dial Books for Young Readers, 1992.

Parks, Rosa, with Gregory J. Reed. *Dear Mrs. Parks: A Dialogue with Today's Youth.* New York: Lee & Low, 1996.

Wilson, Camilla. *Rosa Parks: From the Back of the Bus to the Front of a Movement.* New York: Scholastic, 2001.

INTERNET SITES

National Civil Rights Museum
http://www.civilrightsmuseum.org/
To learn about this museum dedicated to the civil rights movement.

Rosa and Raymond Parks Institute for Self Development
http://www.rosaparksinstitute.org/
For information about this organization and its ongoing work.

Rosa Parks: How I Fought for Civil Rights
http://teacher.scholastic.com/rosa/sitting-down.htm
Includes an interview with Parks.

Time Magazine's "Heroes and Icons of the Twentieth Century"
http://www.time.com/time/time100/heroes/profile/parks01.html
A lively account of Rosa Parks' stand against injustice.

INDEX

About the Author

In addition to authoring thirteen books for young readers, **Marc Tyler Nobleman** has written for *The Great American History Quiz* program on the History Channel and for several children's magazines, including *Nickelodeon* and *Highlights for Children*. He is also a cartoonist whose single panels have appeared in over seventy periodicals, including the *Wall Street Journal*, *Forbes*, *Harvard Business Review*, and *Better Homes and Gardens*.